The Oxford C

Using Data

Developing Writing

Kate Williams

© Oxford Centre for Staff Development 1996

Published by
THE OXFORD CENTRE FOR STAFF DEVELOPMENT
Oxford Brookes University
Gipsy Lane
Headington
Oxford
OX3 0BP

All rights reserved. Except for the quotation of short passages for the purposes of criticism and review, no part of this publication may be reproduced, stored in a retrieval system, or transmitted in any form or by any means, electronic, mechanical, photocopying, recording or otherwise, without the prior permission of the publisher.

Developing Writing – Using Data ISBN 1 873576 37 4
British Library Cataloguing-in-Publication Data. A catalogue record for this book is available from the British Library.

Designed in 10 on 12.5 pt Palatino and Helvetica by Thomas Nicolaou

Printed in Great Britain by
Oxonian Rewley Press Ltd
Oxford

Printed on paper produced from sustainable forests.

Contents

1	**Words and numbers**	**5**
	1.1 Introduction	5
	1.2 How to use the guide	6
2	**Strategic thinking**	**8**
	2.1 Ask key questions	8
	2.2 Ask questions about other people's data	10
3	**Glimpsing the process**	**11**
	3.1 Gathering data	12
	3.2 Analysing data	15
	3.3 Select key strands	16
	3.4 Interpreting data	17
	3.4.1 Tables and words	17
	3.4.2 Charts and words	18
	3.4.3 A closer look at tables	19
	3.5 Feedback on activities	20
4	**Presenting data** **Workshop 1 : An Apple a Day ...?**	**22**
	4.1 Drawing pie charts	22
	4.2 Drawing bar charts	25
	4.3 Drawing histograms	27
	4.4 How to draw and present charts	30
	4.5 Feedback on activities	31
5	**Interpreting data and presenting information** **Workshop 2 : Education in figures**	**33**
	5.1 Getting information from a table	33
	5.2 Using graphs	34
	5.3 Using bar charts	35
	5.3.1 A component bar chart	35
	5.3.2 A simple bar chart	36
	5.4 Using pie charts	39
	5.5 Case study: Focus on education in figures	40
	5.6 Feedback on activities	41
6	**Figures, facts and interpretation** **Workshop 3: The honourable lady was being selective**	**43**
	6.1 Has the government spent 'more'?	44
	6.2 Has average income increased?	47
	6.3 Who are the poor?	50
	6.4 Are some types of family more likely to be poor?	55
	6.5 Feedback on activities	58

Words and numbers

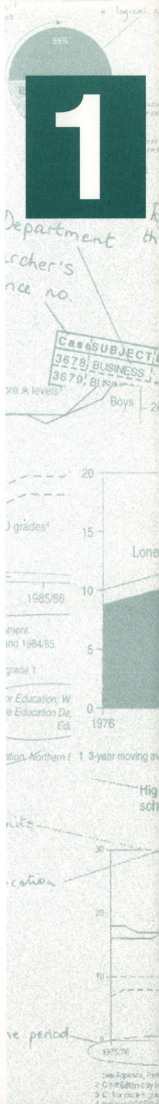

1.1 Introduction

You may be wondering what a guide on using data is doing in a series of guides on writing.

It is here because the ability to make sense of figures and to explain – in words – what you think is important about them is a form of literacy in itself, and a powerful one at that. You can explain numerical data in

- tables and words
- charts and words

– but you always need words: figures do not speak for themselves.

'We go out to find good scientists and by definition that means they can communicate technical information using graphs and tables very well. Where they fall down is linking the data to make a persuasive case.'

(John Hume, director of human resources at Glaxo Research and Development, quoted in The Guardian, 11 July 1994)

This guide is designed to help you make the link between data and words. It is also designed for the data-phobe, to make information in tables and charts accessible to people who are more comfortable with words. You need to be able to explain figures, comment on them, and take issue with them, as you would with any other piece of text. If you don't do it for yourself, other people will. Politicians do it all the time:

Ms Corston: Is the Prime Minister aware that 'Social Trends 1994', a Government publication, reveals that as a direct consequence of Tory Government policy since 1979 the average disposable income of the richest 20 per cent of households has increased by £6,000 a year while the 20 per cent of households at the bottom of the income scale have had their average disposable income cut by £3,000 a year? Does that not reveal the hypocrisy of the Prime Minister's professed commitment to creating a nation at ease with itself?

The Prime Minister: The hon. lady was being selective in what she said – *[Interruption]* She was selective from the report. The net disposable income of people at all ranges of income has increased and the proportion of total tax take paid by those on top incomes has increased, not been reduced.

(Hansard Oral answers 22 February 1994)

Who is right? From reading reports of exchanges, or even the text of the speeches, it is impossible to say. You can see from this short extract two techniques adopted by people who use statistics to support their case. They are

- **selective** in the facts they use
- **precise** in their references and language.

If you want to find out what the debate is about, to form your own view about the merits of the arguments of the different parties, you have to go to the statistics yourself – which we do in Chapter 6 of this guide. You need to be able to

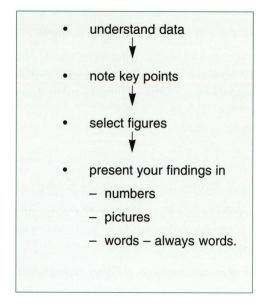

In short, you need to be able to read and interpret figures so you can form your own opinions based on firm evidence, and, of course, present this data to your audience in a form that gets across your message to them clearly and memorably.

The importance of being able to do this has not been lost on people who design higher education courses: many courses now expect you to show some familiarity with the forms and uses of data, even if you did not think you were signing up for work with figures a couple of years ago. This guide is designed to talk you through this process.

1.2 How to use the guide

Make intelligent use of the Contents page, and flick through to find the sections best suited to your purpose right now. You will find the following chapters.

2 Strategic thinking

is about asking yourself questions in a systematic way to clarify your task and your approach to it.

3 Glimpsing the process

aims to track the process of generating your own data and making sense of it.

Chapters 4, 5, and 6 take the form of three workshops involving practical activities. There is a clear hierarchy of complexity in these workshops. You may be confident in working with figures, and opt to start with Workshop 3, but if you are not, start with the basic data presentation in Workshop 1.

4 Workshop 1:   Presenting data

is a practical step-by-step demonstration of how to draw pie charts, bar charts and histograms. Since you are asked to do the tasks, allow time for this. The material for this is a survey of attitudes to health and lifestyles – *An Apple a Day* ...?

5 Workshop 2:   Interpreting data and presenting information

The context is a critical look at government statistics on trends in education, *Education in figures*. It builds on the experience in Workshop 1, and sets a series of practical tasks in interpreting and presenting data. It is worth doing the activities, so again, allow time. The chapter ends with a suggestion for a written assignment – a case study.

6 Workshop 3:   Figures, facts and interpretation

This workshop takes a closer look at some of the statistics on which detailed exchanges between politicians are based. *'The honourable lady was being selective . . . '* focuses on exchanges between Jean Corston MP and John Major PM on the impact of government policies on our society. In this workshop, the emphasis is on how statistics can be used to support a point of view – or different points of view.

This seems like a logical order from an author's point of view, but it may not seem so to you. You will have different priorities and concerns, so your approach will be different. Move around the guide as you want to.

2 Strategic thinking

Chapters 2 and 3 track the process you are embarking on when you set out to produce your own data. Below is a summary of the processes outlined in the two chapters:

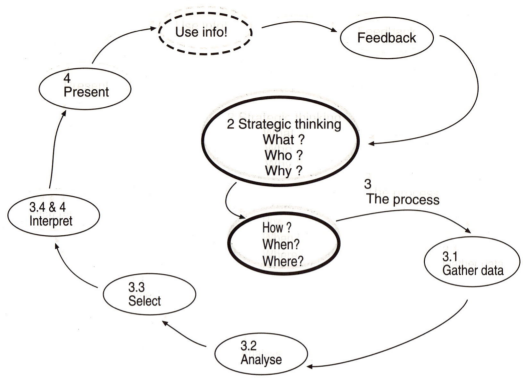

2.1 Ask key questions

Before you set out on an inquiry, you need to be absolutely clear about what you need to produce at the end. If you are generating your own data, you are likely to be setting yourself a task, so you need to ask yourself questions until you have your inquiry in sharp focus.

It can help to start with standard prompt questions:

- **What** area do I want to look into? What exactly do I want to research?

(Check: do I have a precise brief or terms of reference? Do I need to define one? What kind of fact-finding is this? A snapshot of what is? An examination of trends? An experiment?)

- **Who** is it about? Who is it for? Who are the subjects? Who is the audience: the actual audience (tutor, seminar group); the hypothetical audience (assignment scenario, client)?

- **Why** am I carrying out the study? What might result from it?

(Check: Is it to fill an information gap? To test a hypothesis? To study cause and effect?)

The next three questions are key to establishing a sound methodology for your inquiry, so that your results can stand up to scrutiny or be challenged on specific grounds. It is also helpful to ask these questions to help to establish a sensible programme of work within the constraints of time, people available, opportunity and so on.

Developing Writing – Using Data

- **How** am I going to do this?

(Check: Generate new data – by observing? Experimenting? A survey? Use existing data?) This is the big question: your detailed answers to the questions how? will establish the design of your research – and the validity of your findings.

- **When?** What is the impact of time and timing on my inquiry? What are the time constraints on me?

- **Where** do I get my data/subjects from? Can I use existing data?

Any data you produce should be labelled with these details so that your readers can see something of your processes. See 'Five essential points' in Section 2.2 below.

Below is a sketch showing how these questions can be used to develop first ideas into a well defined project and an action plan. The examples are Study 1: *Student attitudes to health,* and Workshop 1: *An Apple a Day...?*

From idea to action

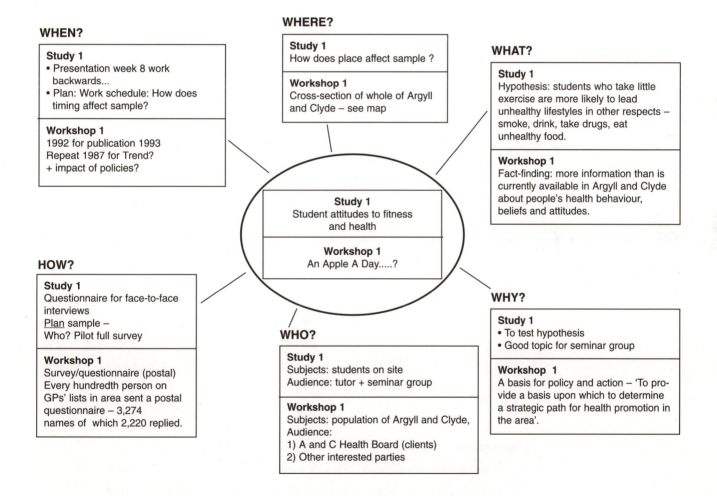

You may find it helpful to see Section 2.3 in Guide 4 in this series, *Writing Reports*, for suggestions on the practicalities of drawing up an action plan.

Strategic thinking

2.2 Ask questions about other people's data

You may have realized that the answers to the key questions for Workshop 1 were not arrived at by eavesdropping on the planning processes of the team of researchers, but by a careful reading of the final report. The answers to these and other questions you might like to ask about their methodology are all recorded there in a reader-friendly way. This is good practice: one you should be careful to adopt yourself, and one you have a right to demand of material presented to you for consumption. Every table and chart should give you all the information you need to make sense of it.

Chart 2A

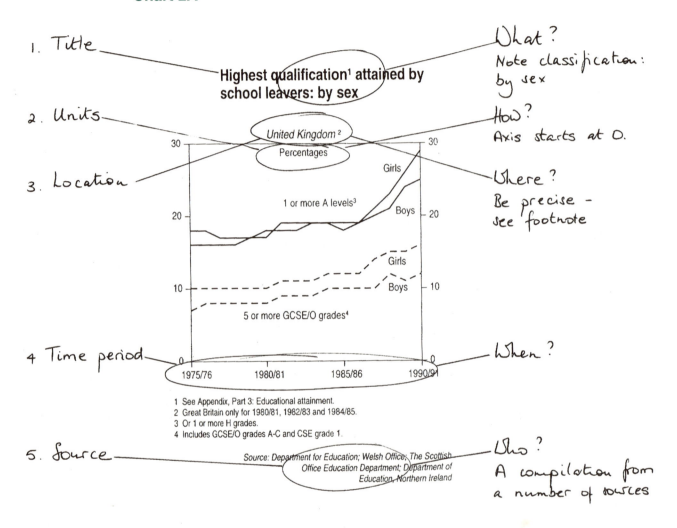

From *Social Trends*, 24 (1994), p. 50.

	Five essential points to look for on tables and charts	
1	**What** is shown – people, objects, events	title
2	**How** they are measured – numbers: thousands, percentages	units
3	**Where** (geographically) the data comes from	location
4	**When** the data was generated/relates to	time period
5	**Who**/which agencies compiled the data	source

The missing question here is 'Why?' It is one to be aware of, even if you can't answer it in relation to other people's data. Someone who works for *Social Trends* asked a question about the school leaving qualifications of boys and girls over the past 20 years which led them to trawl through four government departments for the data for the answer (see 'Source'). Often it is the invisible question, but one which sets the framework of the whole study.

10   *Developing Writing – Using Data*

Glimpsing the process

This chapter outlines the remaining stages in the process of generating and interpreting your own data.

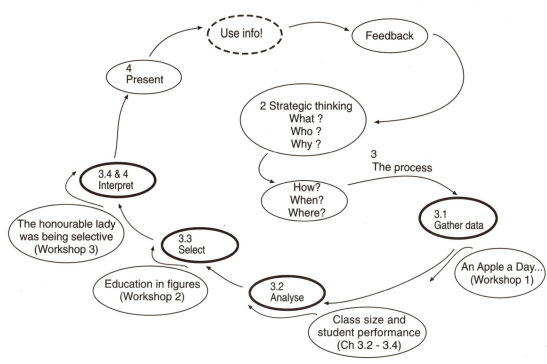

You can see from the diagram how the studies considered in this guide start from different points in the inquiry process. *An Apple a Day . . .?* (Workshop 1, Chapter 4), a professional survey of attitudes to lifestyle and health in Argyll and Clyde, needed to **gather data** that did not exist. The researchers had to start at the beginning of the process and generate their own data by means of a questionnaire. The skill of devising questions that give you the information you need is considered in Section 3.1.

Class size and student performance, also a professional study, is the main focus of Chapter 3. This investigation is based on figures routinely compiled by a university registry. The figures were the raw data which the researcher, Lisa Lucas, had to **analyse (Section 3.2)** for her study. She then had to **select key strands (3.3)** of data, before she moved on to **interpret (3.4)** her observations. Finally she was able to present her findings as useful information. Many thanks to Lisa for her permission to model the figures used here on her actual research into class size and student performance. All figures and course details shown here are, however, fictitious.

The workshops (Chapters 4, 5 and 6) pick up from this point and give you the opportunity to practise these skills. The focus in Workshop 1 is how to present information; in Workshop 2, on how to select, interpret and present key aspects of information contained in government statistics; and in Workshop 3, you are asked to spot how others (politicians) select and interpret figures to convey their own particular messages.

3.1 Gathering data

Is first-hand information-gathering a course requirement? If not, you may find that raw data you can use has already been compiled by someone else. If this is so, find it, skip this section and go to Section 3.2.

If you do decide to gather your own data, you may be aiming for

- a fact-finding **snapshot** of what is – via a **survey** or through **observation**
- measurement of **change** over time
- a study of **cause and effect** by deliberately changing one element in a situation – an **experiment.**

Guide 3, *Scientific and Technical Writing*, shows how to design and use tables and graphs for these purposes.

This section is concerned only with the first of these – the wording of questions for use in a survey; here your use of language is crucial to the outcome of your data-gathering.

Wording a questionnaire

You've done your thinking. You've decided on

- your population – the group you want to study
- how you are going to select a representative sample – a sample with the same characteristics as the population
- how you will collate your answers.

Now you need to design your questionnaire. Consider the points and examples below.

Be clear and precise

Ask short, direct questions. Ask only one question at a time and avoid ambiguous words.

DON'T ASK:

Do you use the local bus service regularly?   Yes/No

This would mean different things to different people. Someone replying 'Yes' might mean 'Yes, every day to go to and from work' or 'Yes, to go swimming every week' or 'Yes, to go to London once a month'.

DO ASK:

Do you use your local bus service

- at least once a day?
- at least once a week?
- at least once a month?
- less than any of the above?
- never?

Don't oversimplify questions in order to save space. You may not get the precise information you need.

Open or closed questions?

Open questions allow the respondent to answer freely.

Example 1

Why did you give up smoking?

Example 2

What do you think about cycle helmets?

You need to have good reasons for using open questions – they are much harder to collate and interpret afterwards. You may want one or two open questions to

- pick up points you had not thought of (at the end perhaps)
- record spontaneous reactions (at the beginning) to a topic you explore later in the questionnaire. Example 2 was used in this way.

Closed questions give the respondents a simple yes/no choice or the option of a range of pre-determined answers. You can see how helpful this is when it comes to collating, interpreting and presenting the results from the examples in Workshop 1, Chapter 4. Most, if not all, questions in a questionnaire should be closed.

Example 1: A Yes / No answer

Would you like to give up smoking?

    Yes

    No

    Not sure

Example 2: Pre-determined replies for quantitative information

About how many cigarettes do you now smoke each day?

    Fewer than 5 _____

    Between 5 and 10 _____

    Between 11 and 20 _____

    Between 21 and 40 _____

    More than 40 _____

or   I only smoke a pipe or cigars

    other tobacco products _____

(from An Apple a Day ....?)

Note the careful wording to avoid overlapping categories:

    Between 11 and 20   NOT   10 – 20

    Between 21 and 40   20 – 40

Example 3: Pre-determined replies for some types of qualitative information

HOW TO ANSWER

On a scale of 1 to 5, where 1 means "definitely disagree" (✗ ✗) and 5 means "definitely agree" (✓✓), circle your responses to the following statements (e.g ✗ ✗ ✗ ? ✓ ✓✓).

1 ② 3 4 5

		✗ ✗	✗	?	✓	✓✓
8	To do well on this module all you need is a good memory.................................	1	2	3	4	5
9	The module seems to encourage us to develop our own academic interests as far as possible..	1	2	3	4	5
10	It seems to me that the syllabus tries to cover too many topics............................	1	2	3	4	5
11	Students have a great deal of choice over how they are going to learn this module........	1	2	3	4	5
12	Staff here seem more interested in testing what we've memorised than what we've understood	1	2	3	4	5

Note the design of these questions. They have

- built-in checks – they ask the same thing in different ways throughout the questionnaire (see questions 8 and 12) and double check the respondents' reliability (see questions 9 and 12)

- safeguards against 'response bias' – the donkey approach to a questionnaire, in which a bored respondent ticks the same box all the way down. A respondent who replies 'strongly agree' to question 9 is likely to reply in a similar way to question 11, but would be less likely to agree strongly to questions 8, 10 and 12. The pattern of replies will give you an idea of how seriously your respondent is taking the questionnaire.

Activity

Can you rephrase an open question to make it a closed question? Study 1 included a number of open questions. Try rephrasing the two below as closed questions.

1 Why did you give up smoking?

2 Have you recently changed your eating habits?
   To what?
   Why?

For comments see the feedback section at the end of the chapter.

3.2 Analysing data

You may be starting your inquiry at this point, working from data routinely collected by others. **Study 2: Class size and student performance**, starts here.

In this study, the basic data compiled by the university registry already exists. The printout looks like this:

Page 19

Percent of students with grades:					MR	DF F/R	FO	Number of students with grades:					MR	DF F/R	FO	No. ent.	Av-er-	Std	module	
A	B+	B	C	P/S	MC	FR	RO	A	B+	B	C	P/S	MC	FR	RO	ered	age	Dev	number	title
6	34	38	13	0	2	6	0	3	16	18	6	0	1	3	0	47	56	11	45374	
4	31	43	17	1	0	0	3	8	69	94	38	3	0	2	6	220	56	7	45364	
1	46	48	4	0	0	0	0	1	32	33	3	0	0	0	0	69	59	5	45413	
3	22	45	27	1	0	1	1	5	42	85	50	2	0	1	2	187	54	7	45431	
20	20	25	19	5	1	8	1	21	21	26	20	5	1	8	1	103	56	14	45444	

The researcher's first task is to identify, from the great bank of data in the registry, the figures that relate to her inquiry:

What is the effect of the size of classes and modules on student performance?

The researcher had to decide which figures to select as a focus for her inquiry. You can see her decisions below:

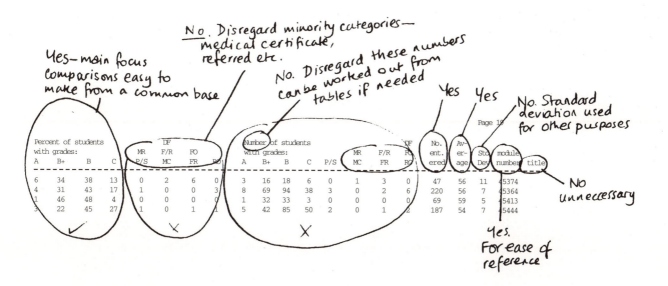

The process of making sense of data, of turning data into useful information, has started.

3.3 Select key strands

The process of selection is a crucial one. Data in itself means nothing. Once you start to select, you also reject: there are topics you don't pursue, comparisons you don't make, trends you ignore. You saw in the exchange between John Major and the Labour MP Jean Corston how each selected the ground on which to do battle . . . ? Well, the process starts here, with the selection of material that suits the researcher's purpose.

The researcher of Study 2 transferred the figures of use to her and produced her own spreadsheet. The data she rejected has now slipped from sight: figures on medical certificates, referrals etc. are there waiting for another researcher to come along with a different question to ask.

The spreadsheet looks like this:

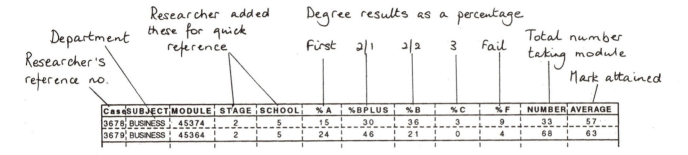

At this point, the research starts to get interesting – patterns start to emerge. As the pages of data build up, you find yourself engaging in what the figures are telling you.

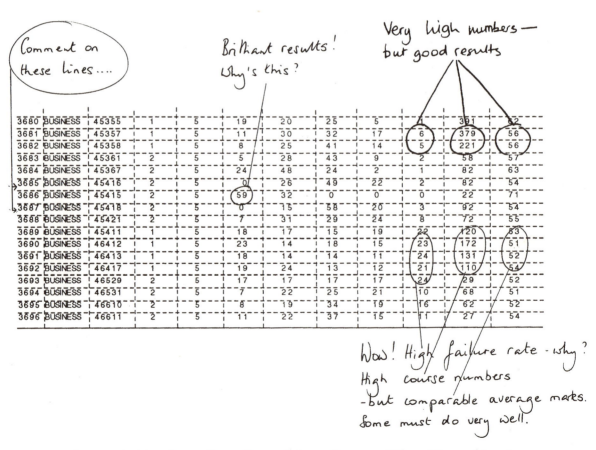

As you start to ask questions of your data, and pursue different lines of inquiry, you begin to manipulate your information – calculate numbers as percentages, add groups together, classify into groups and so on. Your data becomes information.

3.4 Interpreting data

At this point you begin to move through the processes, to

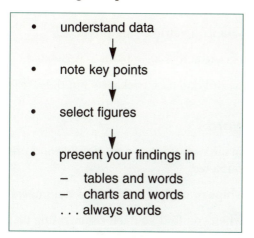

Any table, even a small one, contains an immense amount of information – more than most charts can convey. You need to explain what you see as important in this mass of information. Some charts can translate a single strand of figures into a visual message, others can present several strands for comparison. Always explain the significance of what you have shown.

3.4.1 Tables and words

When the key points you have noted depend on **specific amounts**, use a table.

Below is the information that Lisa, in her research into class size and student performance in Study 2, wanted to convey.

The words

The first sentence links the discussion to the previous point.

> While the differences in average mark are not large for modules of different enrolments, there are wide differences in the proportion of students receiving different grades (corresponding to degree classifications). It can be seen from Table 3A that, while 42.4% of students in modules of 10–20 gained good grades (A or B+, corresponding to a 1st and 2:1 degree), only 33.1% of students in modules of over 70 did so, and that, while 19.9% of students in modules of 10–20 gained poor grades (C or F, corresponding to a 3rd class degree and fail), 24.8% in modules of over 70 did so.

The table

Table 3A   **Module enrolment and student grades at Deseworth University, 1984–94 (n = 6075)**

Module enrolment	%A	%B+	%B	%C	%F
10–20	11.6	30.6	32.9	14.4	5.7
21–30	10.7	30.3	33.8	14.6	5.9
31–40	9.7	29.9	34.4	14.6	5.9
41–50	8.6	29.1	36.4	15.3	6.0
51–60	8.9	27.4	35.7	16.2	7.0
61–70	8.3	26.7	34.5	16.5	7.5
70+	8.7	24.9	37.4	17.7	7.3

(columns grouped under *Grade*)

Glimpsing the process

You can see the translations Lisa has made from the spreadsheet printout on p.16:

- numbers of students enrolled on each module have been classified into ranked categories
- only the key data – grades awarded – are presented
- an average for each grade across all subjects is presented.

All this thanks to a powerful database package – but the researcher made the decisions.

3.4.2 Charts and words

Charts are derived from tables to convey a memorable and precise message. Use a chart when the key points you noted

- depend on **relationships** or comparisons between numbers
- are **non-specific** – when you find yourself commenting on trends or patterns. You might use words such as 'increased markedly', 'declines', 'levelled off'.

Activity

The chart

Look back to the chart in Section 2.2, 'Highest qualification attained by school leavers'.

The words

These are for you to provide, based on your answers to the questions below.

1. Describe the trend in the percentages of young people leaving school since 1976 with a) 5 or more GCSE/O grades b) 1 or more A levels.

2. How does the performance of boys and girls compare over this time in a) GCSE/O level b) A level?

3. Look back at your answers and ring the words you used to describe trends and relationships between numbers. What bearing has this on the form in which the data was presented?

Check your responses with comments in the feedback section at the end of the chapter.

3.4.3 A closer look at tables

> **Activity**
>
> On the following table
>
> - identify and mark the five information points to look for on tables and charts (see Section 2.2)
> - note the other reader-friendly features of a well drawn table
> - supply the words – based on your answers to the three questions below.

1 Title

Table 3B Destination of first degree graduates

Eye-friendly layout

2 Units

Great Britain — Percentages and thousands

- figures for final comparison in vertical columns, not rows
- columns not too far apart
- helpful horizontal rules

3 Location

4 Time period

	Year of graduation			
	1983	1986	1988	1991
United Kingdom employment [1]	48	53	55	44
Further education or training	21	19	18	20
Believed unemployed	10	7	5	10
Overseas graduates leaving United Kingdom	4	3	4	6
Not available for employment	2	2	3	4
Overseas employment [2]	2	2	2	3
Destination not known	13	14	12	13
All first degree graduates (=100%) (thousands)	105	112	117	131

1 Permanent and temporary
2 Home Students

Brain-friendly figures

- rounded to 2 effective digits
- presented in ranked order – biggest top
- thousands and percentages for translations and calculations

5 Source

Source: Department for Education

From *Social Trends*, 24 (1994), p.49.

> 1 What percentage of graduates went straight into employment in a) 1988 b) 1991? Express this difference in thousands. Can you suggest a reason for the difference?
>
> 2 How many more graduates were 'believed unemployed' in 1991 than in 1988? Express this a) as a percentage b) as a proportion c) in absolute numbers.
>
> 3 Describe the trend in graduate employment, unemployment and continued studies you observe over the time period covered by the table.

If you get interested in data, you should find yourself formulating questions that take you beyond the data in front of you. Jot down one question you'd like to research – given the time and opportunity ...

Compare your comments with those in the feedback section at the end of the chapter.

This chapter has tracked the emergence of powerful information from useless data. The process of defining your purpose, and selecting strands of data useful to it, continues through the presentation of information and into the world of action and debate.

3.5 Glimpsing the process: feedback on activities

3.1: Wording a questionnaire: Activity

The researchers for An Apple a Day ...? wanted the same information. This is how they worded their questions:

Question 1

Here are some of the reasons that people have given for giving up smoking. Which of them were important in your decision to stop smoking?

Please tick one box for each reason

	Important	Not Important	Not sure
	1	2	3
To improve fitness	☐	☐	☐
To prevent disease and ill-health	☐	☐	☐

and so on . . . .

Question 2

They used a series of four questions to get the same information in a closed question format, starting with this one:

12   Do you think you eat too much, too little, or about the right amount of the following foods? Please tick one of the boxes for each kind of food.

	Too much	Too little	About right	Not sure	Do not eat
	1	2	3	4	5
Fish	☐	☐	☐	☐	☐
Poultry (chicken, turkey etc)	☐	☐	☐	☐	☐

and so on . . . .

The lead question for the remaining three are given below. You may like to work out the structure for recording the answers to each.

13   Are you eating a different diet from this time last year?

14   If you have changed your diet in the past 12 months, please specify the changes.

15   What was the main reason for changing your diet?

Questions like these take up a lot of space – but are worth it if you want precise quantifiable information.

3.4.2: Charts and words: Activity

You will probably have noted these points.

1. There has been a **steady improvement** in the qualifications of young people leaving school: the proportion leaving with five or more GCSE/O levels has **increased** by about 5% since 1976. The proportion of young people gaining one or more A level or equivalent was **fairly static** at around 18% until 1987, since when the proportion of better qualified school leavers of both sexes has **increased markedly.**

2. A higher proportion of girls than boys have left school with five or more GCSE/O levels throughout the period, and the gap has **widened slightly** in the last few years. There has been a **marked increase** in the numbers of both boys and girls leaving school with at least one A level since 1987. Girls overtook boys at this point; the **increase is sharp and sustained**, and reached almost 30% in 1991, whereas for boys the increase shows signs of **levelling off**, reaching 25% in 1991.

3. From the number of words in bold italics, you can see why a graph was chosen to show trends and relationships.

3.4.3: A closer look at tables: Activity

1. In 1988, 55% (64,350) of graduates went straight into employment, compared with 44% (57,640) in 1991, a difference of about 7000 – less than you might have thought from the 11% drop in graduates going into employment. This is because the total number of graduates has increased by 14,000 in those three years. Evidently the increase in unemployment in the country as a whole has affected graduates too.

2. 10% of graduates were 'believed unemployed' in 1991, double the 5% of 1988. This is more than double in actual numbers – 13,100 in 1991 as against 5850 in 1988 because of the increased size of the cohort.

3. A steadily increasing percentage of graduates went straight into employment between 1983 and 1988, when it peaked at 55%. Correspondingly fewer continued in education and training, or were unemployed. In 1991, this was reversed: 11% fewer went into employment on graduation than in 1988, more stayed in education and training, and the percentage believed unemployed doubled.

A question: what kinds of jobs do graduates go into now compared with 1983? Are more temporary, or in occupations not traditionally regarded as for graduates?

Glimpsing the process

4 Presenting data

Workshop 1: An Apple a Day . . .?

This short workshop shows simple and effective ways of presenting the results of a survey in a final report. The survey set out to investigate people's attitudes to health and lifestyles. The questionnaire included questions on smoking and drinking habits. These are the topics you are asked to work on in this chapter.

The researchers used

- pie charts
- bar charts
- histograms

to show the breakdown of their results. One example of each of these charts is taken from the published report. You are asked to draw another of each to the same model. This is a practical activity, so give yourself time for it.

The originals are reproduced at the end of the chapter in the feedback section.

4.1 Drawing pie charts

Below you have

- the survey question (closed format)
- the results to each part of the question totalled
- the translation of this into a percentage
- the pie chart, and the brief commentary on the findings.

HOW MANY PEOPLE SMOKE?

The question	The answers	The percentage
Which of the following best describes you?		
I smoke daily	656	29.8
I smoke occasionally	79	3.6
I used to smoke daily but do not smoke at all now	414	18.8
I used to smoke occasionally (less than daily) but do not smoke at all now	132	6
I have never smoked	889	40.4
	2170	98.6

22   Developing Writing – Using Data

We first asked the 2,200 people in the survey whether they smoked, and if so how often. Here are their replies.

The chart

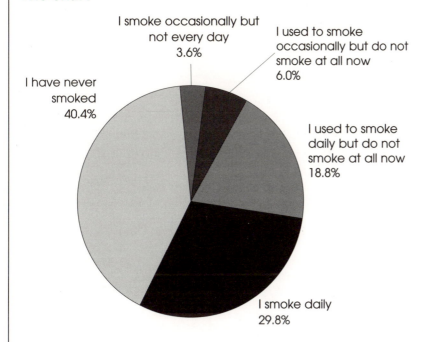

The words

IN ROUND TERMS

- a third of the adults in the area smoke daily or occasionally
- a quarter of the adults in the area used to smoke but no longer do so
- and two-fifths of the adults in the area have never smoked

These proportions of smokers are a little higher than national figures obtained through the General Household Survey – an ongoing survey carried out among about 2,000 adults in Great Britain. In the 1990 survey, 31% of men who were interviewed and 29% of the women said that they smoked regularly or occasionally. This compares with 35% of men and 33% of women in this study.

HOW MANY PEOPLE DRINK?

This time, you do the work! Overleaf you have

- the question from the survey questionnaire
- the numbers of responses to each part of the question totalled.

It is for you to

- translate the totals into percentages
- draw the pie chart
- write the comments.

Don't worry if the numbers are not exact. Where numbers are rounded there is always a small discrepancy, unless you use a graphics pack – in which case it will include decimal points automatically.

Presenting data

The question	The answers	The percentage
How often do you drink alcohol?		
Every day	99	
On five or six days a week	64	
On three or four days a week	238	
On one or two days a week	621	
Less than once a week	693	
I don't drink alcohol at all	469	
	2184	100

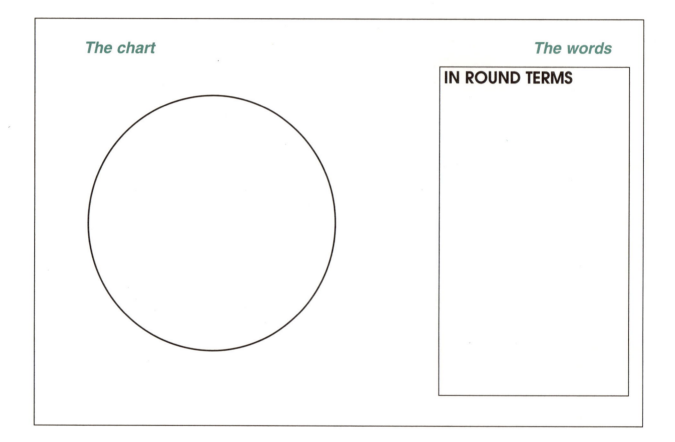

The chart

The words

IN ROUND TERMS

About pie charts ...

Pie charts have an immediate visual impact, so the main features stand out at a glance, even if you forget the exact numbers – which should always be given. Since the whole pie adds up to 100% (or near enough), pie charts are good for showing

- proportion – how a whole divides up
- how proportions change in relation to each other (two or more pies side by side).

Pie charts do not, of course, give any indication of the size of the cake itself.

When you draw pies

- Use round figures.
- Make sure the whole adds up to 100% (or near enough).
- Use a logical order for numbers – often descending order of size.
- If you use more than one pie (for comparison), start each one with the largest measurement at the same point on the pie face: 12 o'clock or 9 o'clock.
- Don't have too many categories. Pies are for showing simple messages, not fine detail. Aim for four; think of six as a maximum.

Always comment on what your chart shows.

4.2 Drawing bar charts

The information in these bar charts was compiled not by direct question and answer, but by collating the results to questions on age and sex with responses to questions on smoking and drinking patterns.

WHICH PEOPLE SMOKE?

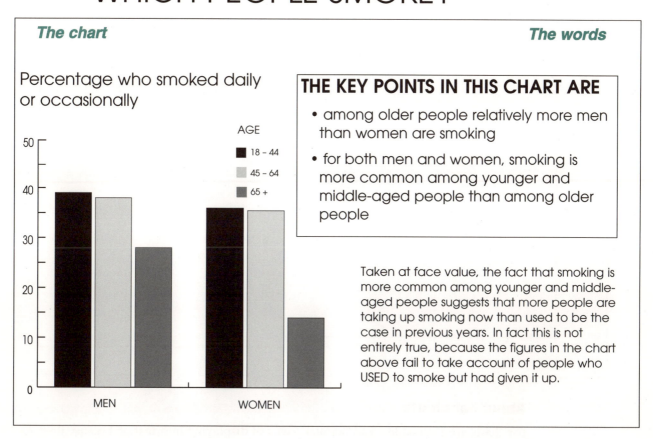

The chart

Percentage who smoked daily or occasionally

AGE
- 18 – 44
- 45 – 64
- 65 +

The words

THE KEY POINTS IN THIS CHART ARE

- among older people relatively more men than women are smoking
- for both men and women, smoking is more common among younger and middle-aged people than among older people

Taken at face value, the fact that smoking is more common among younger and middle-aged people suggests that more people are taking up smoking now than used to be the case in previous years. In fact this is not entirely true, because the figures in the chart above fail to take account of people who USED to smoke but had given it up.

Presenting data   25

WHICH PEOPLE DRINK?

Draw a similar bar chart to show the percentage of men and women who drink alcohol in the three age groups. Then write your comments.

The people	The percentage
Men	
18–44	90
45–64	85
65+	70
Women	
18–44	85
45–64	75
65+	37

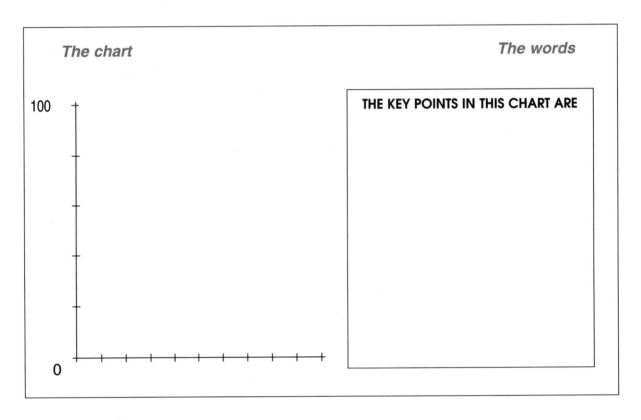

About bar charts

Bar charts are a versatile – and popular – way of displaying information because they are effective in showing

- different totals, either as percentage (as here) or number totals
- changes in totals over a period of time
- comparisons between totals
- the composition of totals
- correlations between two sets of measurements.

Developing Writing – Using Data

When you draw bar charts

- Start the number axis at 0.
- Put the bars in a logical order where the order is not obvious.
- Think about how you might use grouped or component bar charts.
- Horizontal or vertical bars? This is a matter of judgement and preference. It is often easier to label horizontal bars clearly: there is more space for the writing.

Always comment on what the chart shows.

4.3 Drawing histograms

Below you have

- the survey question (closed format)
- the results to each part of the question totalled
- the translation of this into a percentage
- the histogram, and the brief commentary on the findings.

HOW MUCH DO PEOPLE SMOKE?

The question	*The numbers*	*The percentage*
About how many cigarettes do you now smoke each day?		
Fewer than 5	51	7
Between 5 and 10	117	16
Between 11 and 20	360	49
Between 21 and 40	140	19
More than 40	7	1
or I only smoke a pipe or cigars other tobacco products	59	8
	734	100

Presenting data

The chart

The words

Of the 2,200 people in the survey, 734 (33.4%) said they smoked daily or occasionally. We asked these 734 smokers how many cigarettes, on average, they smoked each day. Here are their replies.

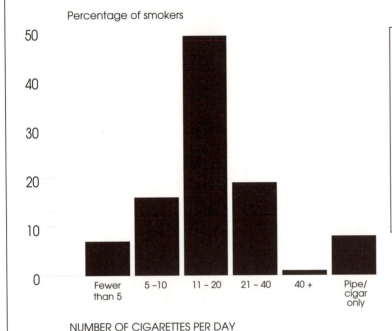

Again, these figures are very close to the national figures obtained through the General Household Survey. In the 1990 survey, the average number of cigarettes smoked each day by those who used them was 17.1 for men and 14.1 for women, compared with an estimated average of 18.2 for men and 15.4 for women in Argyll and Clyde.

HOW MUCH DO PEOPLE DRINK?

Again, this chart is for you to draw – a histogram.

Below is an explanation of the figures you will be using:

Of the 2,200 people in the survey, 1,712 (78%) said they drank alcohol, even if only occasionally. We asked these 1,712 drinkers how many drinks they had, on average, on the days when they drank. By multiplying the NUMBER OF DAYS IN THE WEEK on which people said they drank by the NUMBER OF DRINKS they consumed on the days they drank, we can obtain an estimate of the amount of alcohol that people drink each week. The consumption is expressed as UNITS.

(An Apple a Day...?)

The results were as follows:

Units consumed per week	Numbers	Percentage
None	469	
1	351	
1–2	308	
3–10	593	
11–20	153	
21–30	108	
31+	87	
No answer	131	
	2200	100

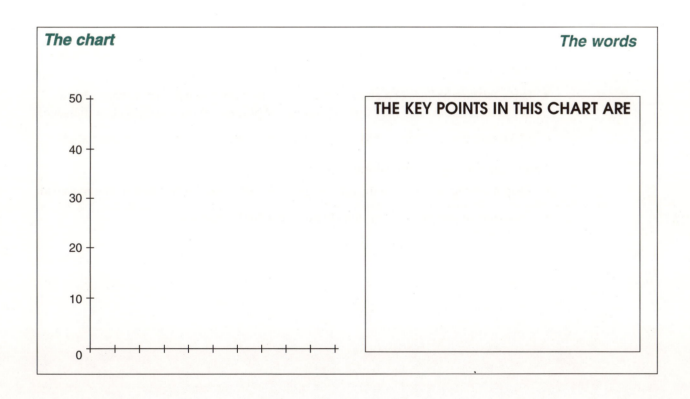

Presenting data   29

About histograms

A histogram is particular form of bar chart with a clearly defined use: to record the frequency with which different measurements occur in a set of data. In other words, while you can select data to present in a bar chart, a histogram records the whole.

When you draw histograms

- Make sure your categories do not overlap (5–10, 11–20, 21–30 etc.).
- Strictly speaking, the width of the bars along the base should represent regular intervals in the data, not groups of various sizes as in the examples here. You will have to judge the accuracy required in your subject.

Always comment on what the chart shows.

4.4 How to draw and present charts: some general points

First, give your reader the essential information they need to make sense of it.

Five essential points to mark on tables and charts

1	**What** is shown – people, objects, events	**title**
2	**How** they are measured – numbers: thousands, percentages	**units**
3	**Where** (geographically) the data comes from	**location**
4	**When** the data was generated/relates to	**time period**
5	**Who**/which agencies compiled the data	**source**

Second, make it easy to read.

- Don't make the charts too big or too small – there is an optimum size so they work with your text and do not dominate it or get lost in it.
- Label sections or lines of a chart on the chart wherever possible rather than using a key at the bottom. This may distract from your purpose of presenting a clear message.
- Make sure the shadings or hatching or colouring you use are clearly differentiated.

Third, make it easy to understand.

- Keep it simple: don't try to include too much information. Draw several charts instead.
- Talk your reader through: figures do not speak for themselves.

4.5 Feedback on activities

The data you were asked to work on was presented as follows in An Apple a Day ...? Note points of similarity and difference with your own work, and the extent to which the two versions do – or do not – tally with the advice in the text.

4.1 Drawing pie charts

HOW MANY PEOPLE DRINK?

We first asked the 2,200 people in the survey how often they drank alcohol. Here are their replies.

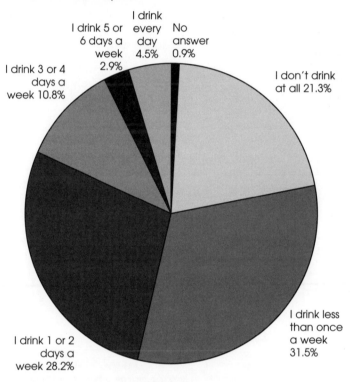

- I drink 5 or 6 days a week 2.9%
- I drink every day 4.5%
- No answer 0.9%
- I drink 3 or 4 days a week 10.8%
- I don't drink at all 21.3%
- I drink 1 or 2 days a week 28.2%
- I drink less than once a week 31.5%

IN ROUND TERMS
- a fifth of the adults in the area say they are abstainers
- almost a third of the adults in the area say they are occasional drinkers (less than once a week)
- just over a quarter of the adults in the area say they are light drinkers (one or two days a week)
- and a fifth of the adults in the area say they are moderate or heavier drinkers (3 or more days a week)

These proportions are very similar to those reported elsewhere. For example, in an identical survey carried out in the Brighton Health District in 1989, 9% said they drank every day (compared with 5% in this survey), 22% said they drank on one or two days per week (compared with 28% in this survey), and 19% said they did not drink at all (compared with 21% in this survey).

Presenting data 31

4.2 Drawing bar chart

WHICH PEOPLE DRINK?

People who drink are not typical of the total adult population. There are differences of age, gender and social class. The chart below illustrates the difference of age. It shows the percentage of men and women in each of three age groups who said they drank alcohol at all, and the average amount of alcohol that they reported drinking each week.

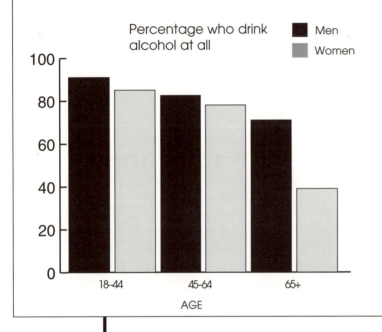

THE KEY POINTS IN THIS CHART ARE

- at all ages, relatively more men than women say they drink alcohol, and the gap between men and women widens with increasing age

- among both men and women, relatively more younger than older people say they drink alcohol. The decline in drinking among older people is more marked for women than for men

4.3 Drawing histograms

HOW MUCH DO PEOPLE DRINK?

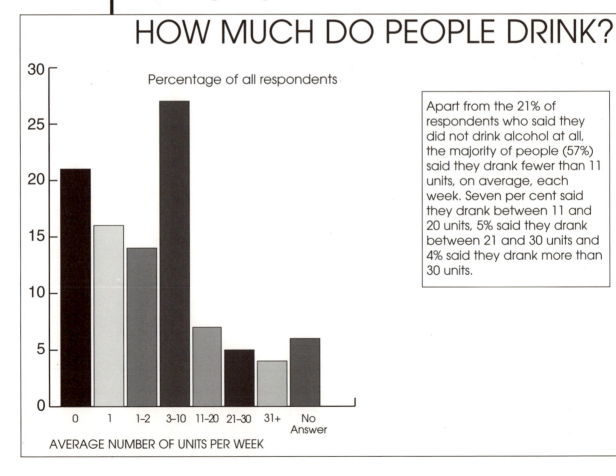

Apart from the 21% of respondents who said they did not drink alcohol at all, the majority of people (57%) said they drank fewer than 11 units, on average, each week. Seven per cent said they drank between 11 and 20 units, 5% said they drank between 21 and 30 units and 4% said they drank more than 30 units.

Interpreting data and presenting information

Workshop 2: Education in figures

This workshop is based on published government statistics showing trends in education, particularly in higher education. In it you are asked to translate data from tables into charts. To do this you need to follow the process:

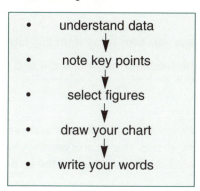

- understand data
- note key points
- select figures
- draw your chart
- write your words

This is a more complex activity than the straightforward presentation of data in Workshop 1. The **In detail** questions are designed to help you understand and interpret the data. Feedback on these and some of the drawing activities is given at the end of the section.

5.1 Getting information from a table

Table 5A Full and part-time students in higher education[1,2]: by sex and type of establishment

United Kingdom   Thousands

	Males					Females				
	1970/71	1975/76	1980/81	1985/86	1991/92[3]	1970/71	1975/76	1980/81	1985/86	1991/92[3]
Full-time and sandwich students										
Universities										
Undergraduates	134	141	157	148	178	59	77	101	108	150
Postgraduates	33	37	34	37	46	10	13	15	17	28
Other[4]										
Undergraduates	107	123	120	146	207	114	123	95	129	211
Postgraduates			7	7	11			6	7	12
All full-time students	274	301	318	339	442	182	214	217	261	400
Part-time students										
Universities										
Undergraduates	3	2	2	5	6	2	2	2	5	8
Postgraduates	15	17	20	22	31	3	5	8	11	23
Open University[5]	14	34	38	43	51	5	22	29	36	48
Other[4]										
Undergraduates	110	115	138	134	144	12	21	42	65	107
Postgraduates			9	12	21			3	5	17
All part-time students	142	168	207	215	253	23	50	86	122	202
All students	416	470	524	553	695	205	264	303	384	602

1 See Appendix, Part 3: Stages of education
2 Excludes students enrolled on nursing and paramedic courses at Department of Health establishments
3 Excludes 2.5 thousand non-university students in Scotland recorded as sex unknown
4 Polytechnics and other higher education establishments
5 Calendar years beginning in second year shown. Excludes short courses students up to 1982/83

From *Social Trends*, 24 (1994), p.47.   Source: Department for Education

Interpreting data and presenting information

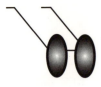

In detail

Identify the essential information about the table – the five points: title, units, location, time period, source.

1. What has the trend been in student numbers over the time period? Look at the 'All students' total, then at full-time students, male and female, and part-time students, male and female.

2. Where have the greatest increases taken place? Look at full-time male/female students in 'universities' (pre-1992), and 'other' (what does this mean?). Look at part-time students, male/female, at 'universities' (pre-1992), 'other' and the Open University.

3. What is the key message you take away from this table?

Check your answers with the feedback section at the end of the chapter.

5.2 Using graphs

Below is a graph showing the increase in numbers of male and female students noted in the key message from the table above. The figures are the totals shown in the bottom row of the table. The words are based on the feedback to the **In detail** questions.

Graph 5B

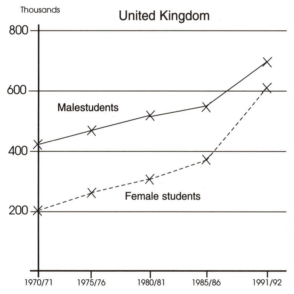

There has been a huge and accelerating increase in student numbers over the past 20 years; about half this increase has taken place over the last six years shown on the graph. Most of this increase has been among women students; while the number of male students has increased by 50%, the number of female students has trebled.

Source: Social Trends (1994).

Draw a graph

Choose two other points, comparisons or trends that emerged in your answers to the **In detail** questions.

You may want to look at

- students in the (old) universities/(new) universities ('Other')
- students taking full-/part-time courses
- students taking OU courses (men/women)
- male/female postgraduate students.

Draw a graph that communicates your message effectively, following the process outlined in sections 5.1 and 5.2.

About graphs

The graph in Section 2.2 (Highest qualification attained by school leavers: by sex) is an example of a well drawn graph.

Graphs are good for

- showing trends – the changes or movement in a measurement over a period of time
- making comparisons – the changes in several measurements over a period of time.

When you draw graphs

- Show your vertical axis from 0 to a point high enough to include your highest value comfortably – unless you have good reason for showing only a narrow range.
- Don't put too many lines on one graph: four is a reasonable maximum.
  Always comment on what the graph shows.

5.3 Using bar charts

5.3.1 A component bar chart

Chart 5C   Full and part time students in further education: by sex

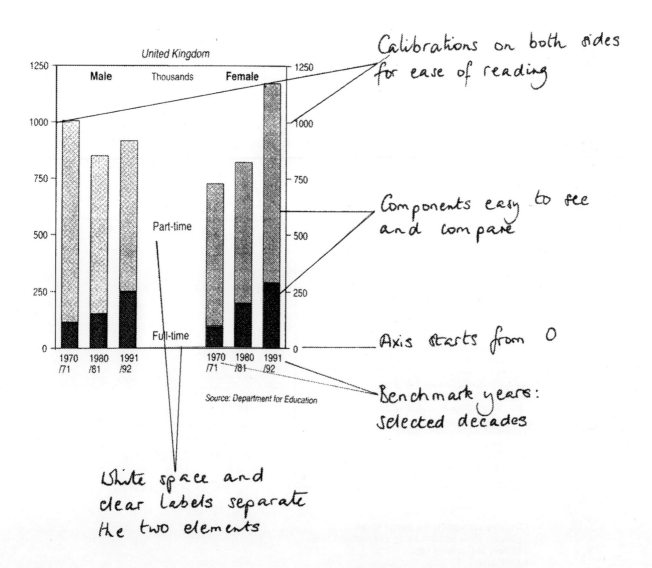

Source: Department for Education

Annotations:
- Calibrations on both sides for ease of reading
- Components easy to see and compare
- Axis starts from 0
- Benchmark years: selected decades
- White space and clear labels separate the two elements

From *Social Trends*, 24 (1994), p. 46.

Interpreting data and presenting information   35

In detail

Note the basic information about the chart – the five points.

1 What do you notice about the numbers of male and female students in
   a) full-time b) part-time further education over the period shown?

2 Where have the greatest changes taken place?

3 Ask a follow-up question.

Check your answers in the feedback section.

Draw a component bar chart

Using the bar chart above as a model, pick out the equivalent figures for higher education from Table 5A on page 33:

- the same benchmark years
- figures for full-time male/female students
- figures for part-time male/female students.

1 Draw a similarly designed component bar chart to show your results.

2 In your own words comment on
   a) what your chart shows
   b) the comparison between trends in further and higher education over the period.

5.3.2 A simple bar chart

Chart 5D Public expenditure[1] on education as a percentage of GNP: international comparison, 1989

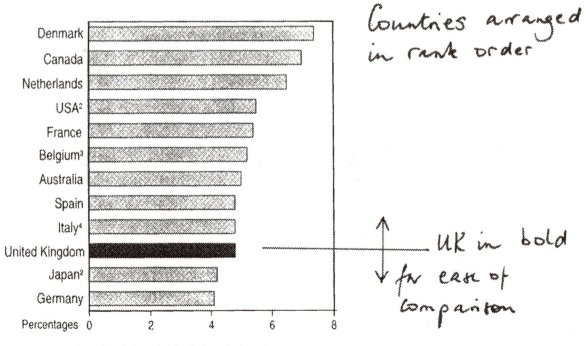

1 Includes subsidies to the private sector.
2 Includes some private funding, but excludes fees.
3 Ministry of Education only.
4 1987 data.

From *Social Trends*, 24 (1994), p. 54.

Source Department of Education

In detail

Make sure you are clear about what the chart shows – check the five points: title, units, location, time period, source.

1. At a glance, what first draws your attention?
2. How would you describe the UK's position in relation to other countries in the percentage of GNP spent on education?
3. Which two countries are ranked below the UK? Which countries spend the highest percentage?
4. Ask a follow-up question.

Check your answers in the feedback section.

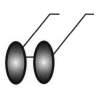

Your summary

From table to chart

The previous bar chart was drawn from a single batch of figures selected from a table like this one:

Table 5E: PUBLIC EXPENDITURE ON EDUCATION (FOR CALENDAR YEAR SHOWN)

	Total public education expenditure[1] as % of GNP	Public Recurrent expenditure[1,2] per capita		HE Recurrent expenditure[1,2] per qualifiers £000s
		Below HE level £	HE £	
	1990	1989		1989
Australia	5.2	250	120	23.0
Belgium[4]	5.1	310	80	14.5
Canada	7.4	460	220	29.3
Denmark	7.5	440	100[5]	26.8
France	5.4	330	60	9.3
Germany, Fed	4.1	240	80	20.1
Italy	5.0	310[7]	50[7]	31.4[7]
Japan[8,9]	4.0	250[7]	30[7]	28.3[10,11]
Netherlands	6.3	290	170	39.3
Spain	4.2	230[12]	40	11.8
Sweden	7.2	410	90	19.2
UK	4.7 (5.0)[13]	330	80	16.2[14]
USA[8,9](a)	5.7	440	160	20.3[11]
(b)[16]		470	130	23.7

Adapted from *Education Statistics for the United Kingdom* (1993)

Interpreting data and presenting information

About this table

This table was designed to store information, not to communicate it. You can tell from

- the number of detailed footnotes (the text of which is omitted)
- the arrangement of the countries, alphabetically for ease of reference, not in ranked order, for ease of communication.

Draw a simple bar chart

Two activities are suggested here to give you practice in drawing bar charts. For how to draw bar charts, see Section 4.2.

1 **'Total public education expenditure as % of GNP'. Select this column from the table above.**

   - Draw a bar chart to show this information.
   - Comment on what it shows.
   - Compare your chart with Chart 5D above. In your summary, include a comparison of the two.

2 **'Public Recurrent expenditure per capita': 'Below HE level' and 'HE'. Select these two columns from Table 5E, study the figures carefully and note the detail.**

   - What general pattern emerges?
   - What do you observe about the range of expenditure on education between the different countries?
   - How do priorities for expenditure (below degree level, and degree level) vary between the countries?
   - How does the UK's pattern and level of expenditure compare with other countries?
   - Display this information in bar chart form. How will you do this?
     - Two simple bar charts, one for each set of figures? Or grouped bar charts?
     - What order will you place the countries in: the same as in (1) above or different? Why?
   - Write your commentary, based on the detail you noted.

5.4 Using pie charts

Three activities are suggested here, to give you practice in drawing pie charts. For how to draw pie charts, see Section 4.1.

> **Draw a pie chart**
>
> **1 Destination of first degree graduates**
>
> Look back to Table 3B, your answers to the **In detail** questions, and the summary you wrote based on these. If this table is new to you, take a few minutes to work through the detail.
>
> i   Draw two pie charts to outline the contrasts between 1988 and 1991. Present these side by side.
>
> ii Write a commentary in which you highlight the key points you want to convey through your charts.
>
> A version of this is given in the feedback section.
>
> **2 Degree results of different modules**
>
> Look back to the extract from the spreadsheet in Section 3.4.1 showing the breakdown of these.
>
> i   Select two modules with a contrasting pattern of results and draw a pie chart for each. Present them side by side.
>
> ii Write your commentary.
>
> **3 Students in higher education**
>
> Look back to Table 5A, and select some figures you think could be helpfully displayed in one or two pie charts. This is not an easy task. Because the numbers here are thousands, and pie charts show percentages, you will have to turn any group of figures you select into percentages.
>
> i   Draw the pie charts.
>
> ii Write your commentary.

5.5 Case study: Focus on education in figures

Which aspects of this study have most interested you? Your task here is to choose a strand of the information presented here, and write it up in the form of a short article (500 words maximum) suitable for publication in a newspaper, magazine or broadsheet of your choice.

Below is a summary of some of the material we have considered, presented in the order in which you find it in the guide. Some suggestions for topics are given in the box, but you may think of others. If you decide to look out some material of your own, so much the better.

You may like to approach the task in this order.

- Decide on the publication you are writing for. Who reads it? Why might they be interested in, or need to know about, your topic?

- Decide on your topic. Be clear about its relevance to your chosen audience.

- Identify relevant sources and key strands within sources.

- Order your material, and write, in a style appropriate to the readership of your publication.

- You may find it helpful to write the body first, then the conclusion, and the introduction last.

- Keep your (imaginary) reader in mind from start to finish. Write for them.

- Give your piece a title.

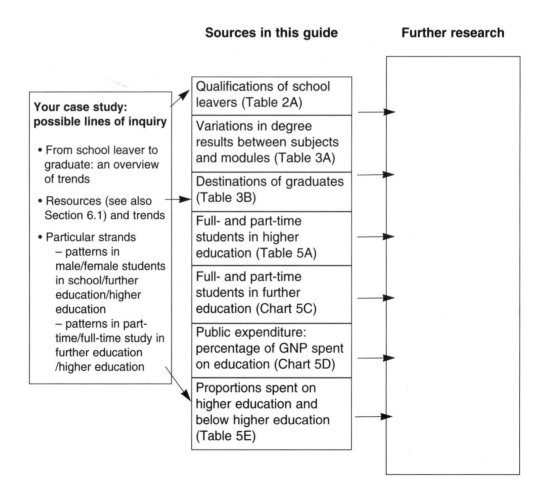

5.6 Feedback on activities in Chapter 5

5.1 In detail: Getting information from a table

Key message: there has been a huge and accelerating increase in student numbers over the past 20 years, especially of women students.

- *The number of female students has trebled, from 205,000 in 1971 to 602,000 in 1992. The overall trebling of female students disguises much more dramatic increases throughout most of the education system:*

    * *trebling in the old universities (from 59,000 to 150,000)*

    * *a tenfold increase of part-time students at the new universities (old polytechnics and higher education colleges) (from 12,000 in 1971 to 124,000 in 1992)*

    * *a tenfold increase in the number of part-time female OU students*

    * *a huge (proportionate) increase in part-time students at the old universities (from 2,000 to 8,000).*

- *The number of male students has increased by 50%, half as much again (416,000 in 1971 to 695,000 in 1992). The 50% overall increase in the numbers of male students also disguises wide variations:*

    * *a comparatively modest increase in numbers at the old universities (about 25%)*

    * *a trebling of OU students*

    * *a doubling in the former polytechnics.*

5.3.1 In detail: A component bar chart

1   *The numbers of students, both male and female, have roughly doubled over the 20-year period. Numbers of full-time female students have risen from about 100,000, somewhat fewer than males in 1970/71, to about 300,000, somewhat more than male students over the 20-year time period. This 'somewhat' is deceptive because of the large steps of the axis: there were about 50,000 more female than male students in 1991/2. The number of part-time male students has decreased considerably over the period, while the number of part-time female students has increased markedly, especially in the 1980s. Overall, part-time students outnumber full-time by about 3:1.*

2   *The greatest change is the overall decline in the numbers of part-time male students, and the significant increase – in both relative and absolute terms – of part-time female students, particularly in the 1980s.*

3   *A question (or two): The decrease in part-time male students is presumably the result of the loss of the apprenticeship system – a consequence of the collapse of work opportunities for the young. What are these young men doing now? Who are the part-time female students? School leavers, or mature women who didn't get the chance in the 1970s?*

5.3.2 In detail: A simple bar chart

My guess is that you had to look twice at the title, and think for a moment about what it means.

Your attention was probably drawn by the UK's low position in the ranking of the percentage of GNP spent on education. The countries with the highest proportion spent are not surprising – but it is surprising to see Japan and Germany at the bottom.

Questions: Do Japan and Germany spend less than other countries on education, or is their GNP higher? Does Japan use industry for training? Has Germany's expenditure been reduced since unification? What was it before?

5.4: Using pie charts

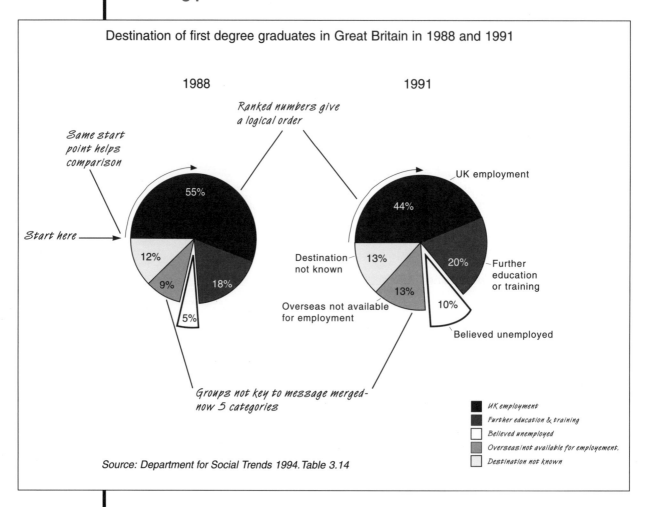

This is my second draft of these pie charts. The first included all the minor categories – distracting and irrelevant to the purpose of the chart, which is to highlight the increase in graduate unemployment. The lift-out section draws attention to this. You could make the chart chattier by including comments.

Figures, facts and interpretation

Workshop 3: The honourable lady was being selective . . .

'It is true – [the] Government has spent more over the last two years. We had to, to help the weak and protect the vulnerable through the recession.'

(*John Major: speech to the Conservative Party Conference, 8 October 1993*)

This comment gives us the terms of reference for this inquiry:

> **Who are the 'weak and vulnerable' in our society? To what extent has the government been successful in protecting these groups over the last 15 years?**

At the end of the workshop, you are asked to write a report in response to this question. In order to approach the fact-finding necessary to answer a question of this sort, you need to ask additional specific questions. Has the government spent 'more'? Has spending been concentrated on the 'weak and vulnerable'? Has inequality of income lessened – or have the rich got richer and the poor poorer? and so on.

This inquiry follows a few of the many strands you could pursue in an examination of this sort. Each double page of the case study contains figures and facts in the form of tables and charts, and interpretations of them in the form of words. The source of the figures is official government statistics, mostly *Social Trends*. The source of the words is exchanges and correspondence between Jean Corston, Labour MP for Bristol East, and John Major, Conservative Prime Minister at the time.

Your task is to form your own views and interpretations of trends in our society. In the process you will need to

- adopt a questioning approach to material on the page (formalized in a **Find out question**)
- show detailed understanding of the data (starting with **In detail questions**)
- express key points in **graphic form** (through drawing charts)
- look closely at **definitions**
- link **assertions** to the **evidence**
- write your own **evaluation** of the arguments and evidence in your response to the **Find out question**.

It should by now be a familiar process:

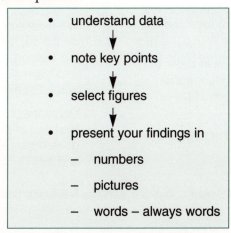

Figures, facts and interpretation   43

6.1 Find out question 1:
i) Has the government spent 'more'?
ii) If so, has the money been spent on the welfare services?

For each of the tables below, note carefully the five essential information points: title, units, location, time period and source. Make a mental note of why this is particularly important here.

FIGURES, FACTS ...

Table 6A

General government expenditure[1]: by function

United Kingdom — £ billion

Function	1981	1986	1990	1991
Defence	12.6	19.1	22.9	27.3
Public order and safety	4.3	6.8	10.9	12.8
Education	14.3	19.3	26.7	29.5
Health	13.4	19.2	27.7	30.9
Social security	31.1	49.9	62.9	73.9
Housing and community amenities	7.1	8.1	7.8	9.1
Recreational and cultural affairs	1.6	2.4	3.7	3.9
Fuel and energy	0.3	-1.2	-3.9	-5.0
Agriculture, forestry and fishing	1.7	2.1	2.6	2.4
Mining, mineral resources, manufacturing and construction	3.6	1.9	1.2	1.7
Transport and communication	4.2	3.7	9.5	6.7
General public services	4.5	6.3	10.7	9.2
Other economic affairs and services	2.9	4.1	6.9	5.5
Other expenditure	15.4	20.7	25.2	19.7
Total expenditure	117.1	162.3	214.8	227.5

1 Includes privatisation proceeds.

Source: Central Statistical Office

From *Social Trends*, 23 (1993).

Table 6B

General government expenditure: by function

United Kingdom — Percentages and £ billion

	1981	1986	1990	1991
Defence[1]	10.8	11.8	9.2	9.7
Public order and safety	3.7	4.2	5.6	5.5
Education	12.2	11.9	12.9	12.7
Health	11.4	11.8	13.7	13.8
Social security	26.6	30.8	32.3	33.1
Housing and community amenities	6.1	5.0	4.0	4.3
Recreational and cultural affairs	1.4	1.5	1.7	1.6
Fuel and energy	0.3	-0.7	-1.5	-0.6
Agriculture, forestry and fishing	1.4	1.3	1.2	1.1
Mining, mineral resources, manufacturing and construction	3.0	1.2	0.7	0.5
Transport and communication	3.6	2.3	3.0	2.5
General public services	3.9	3.9	4.9	4.8
Other economic affairs and services	2.5	2.5	2.0	2.0
Other expenditure	13.1	12.7	9.4	9.1
Total expenditure (= 100%) (£ billion)	117.1	162.3	228.3	254.1

1 Includes contributions by other countries towards the United Kingdom's cost of the gulf conflict – £2.1 billion in 1991

Source: Central Statistical Office

From *Social Trends*, 24 (1994).

In detail A

1 By roughly how much has expenditure increased over the time period shown?

2 Of this total, how much was spent in 1991 on the six functions listed at the top of the list? Express this as a total and as a percentage.

3 List these six major functions in order of the size of the increase in government expenditure on them between 1981 and 1991.

4 Why do you think 'Fuel and energy' show minus figures?

In detail B

1 By how much (in £billions) has government expenditure increased from 1981 to 1991? In 1991–2, does it continue to increase at the same rate?

2 What percentage of the whole was spent on the six functions listed at the top of the table in 1991? How much (in £billions) was spent on housing and education?

3 Do all these six major functions show an increase in the proportion the government spent on them between 1981 and 1991?

Check your responses to the **In detail** questions with the feedback comments at the end of the chapter.

and INTERPRETATION

One point should strike you forcefully: the different pictures of the pattern of government spending that emerge from the two tables. The charts you draw from the figures simply make this difference visible – like this:

Message 1: From 1981 to 1991 spending on education has . . .

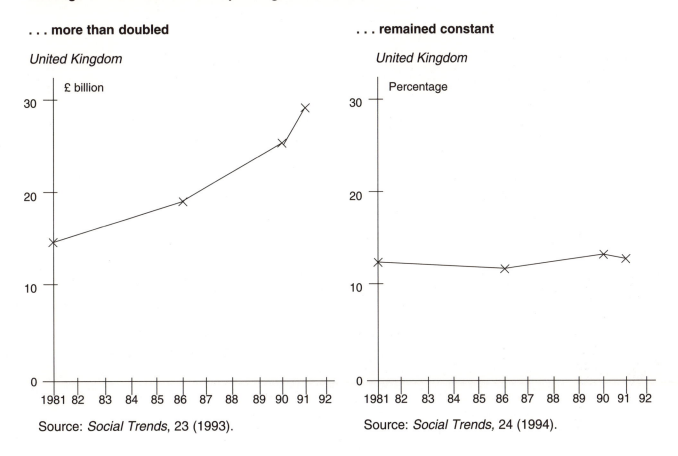

Source: *Social Trends*, 23 (1993).   Source: *Social Trends*, 24 (1994).

Try this yourself.

Figures, facts and interpretation

Message 2: From 1981 to 1991 spending on housing has ...

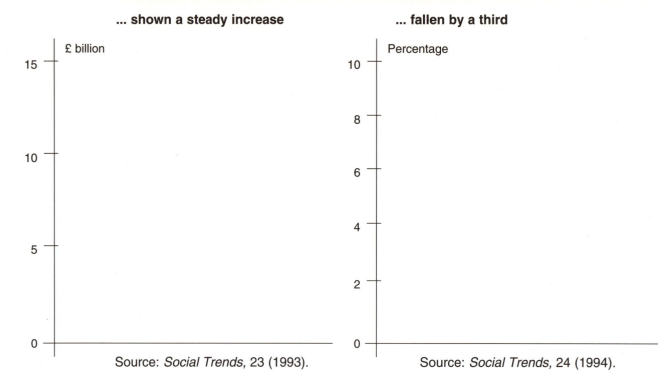

Source: *Social Trends*, 23 (1993).   Source: *Social Trends*, 24 (1994).

'The honourable lady was being selective ....' countered John Major to Jean Corston's attack on his government's record, quoted on p. 5 of this guide. In his reply, he too was selective.

> **Your words**
>
> In your answer to **Find out question 1**, put your own interpretation on the figures presented on this page. Draw on your answers to the **In detail** questions, and any graphs you have drawn.

6.2 Find out question 2:
'For all income bands recorded in Social Trends average income has increased.' (John Major) True or false?

FIGURES, FACTS

Table 6C Real median income[1]: by quintile group

United Kingdom						Indices (1979 bottom fifth=100)
	Quintile groups of individuals					Average of all indivi- duals
	Bottom fifth	Next fifth	Middle fifth	Next fifth	Top fifth	
Net income before housing costs						
1979	100	137	173	220	300	192
1981	98	133	171	218	310	192
1987	104	147	197	258	392	231
1988 – 1989	104	153	210	278	417	247
1990 – 1991	103	156	216	293	446	260
Net income after housing costs						
1979	100	138	177	226	312	197
1981	96	135	174	225	323	196
1987	99	143	200	267	406	236
1988 – 1989	100	153	217	289	438	255
1990 – 1991	97	155	222	304	467	267

1 The unit of analysis is the individual and the income measure is net equivalent household income. See Appendix, Part 5: Households Below Average income and Equivalisation scales.

Source: Department of Social Security

From *Social Trends*, 24 (1994), p. 77.

In detail

Note the five essential information points in the table and check you understand them: title ('median income'?), units ('indices'?), location, time period, source.

1. Taking the 'before housing costs' measurement, by how much have the incomes of a) the poorest 20% b) the richest 20% increased since 1979?

2. Taking the 'after housing costs' figures, how have the incomes of a) the poorest 20% b) the richest 20% moved since 1979?

3. How would you describe the income of the poorest 20% relative to the rest of the population in a) 1979 b) 1991?

4. Ask a question that goes beyond the data.

   For comments, see the feedback section.

Figures, facts and interpretation

FIGURES, FACTS

Table 6D Distribution of disposable household income[1]

United Kingdom						Percentages
	Quintile groups of individuals					
	Bottom fifth	Next fifth	Middle fifth	Next fifth	Top fifth	Total
Net income before housing costs						
1979	10	14	18	23	35	100
1981	10	14	18	23	36	100
1987	9	13	17	23	39	100
1988 – 1989	8	12	17	23	40	100
1990 – 1991	7	12	17	23	41	100
Net income after housing costs						
1979	10	14	18	23	35	100
1981	9	14	18	23	36	100
1987	8	12	17	23	40	100
1988 – 1989	7	12	17	23	41	100
1990 – 1991	6	12	17	23	43	100

1 The unit of analysis is the individual and the income measure is net equivalent household income. See Appendix, Part 5: Households Below Average income and Equivalisation scales.

Source: Department of Social Security

From *Social Trends*, 24 (1994), p. 77.

Activity

1   Check the five essential points and ask yourself 'In detail' questions to clarify its message.

2   Decide whether you will take the figures for 'before housing costs' or 'after housing costs'. Draw two pie charts to show the distribution of income between the five quintiles in 1979 and 1991. Note key points to include in the **Your words** section opposite.

and INTERPRETATION

Dear Jean

Thank you for your letter of 23 February, following our exchange in the House the day before.

Your question referred to *Social Trends* 1994 and to the income growth of the poorest 20 per cent of the population. *Social Trends* show that the income of this group increased by 3 per cent before housing costs. My reply was therefore entirely accurate.

Social Trends also showed that real disposable income in 1992 was at its highest ever; that pensioners' income was up 35 per cent in the decade following 1981; and that for all income bands recorded in *Social Trends* average income increased.

(11 April 1994)

Dear Prime Minster

Thank you for your reply of 11 April to my letter of 23 February, ...

The matter is of such huge importance in assessing the economic and social development of the nation - and its policies - that politicians have a responsibility to reach agreement about what the evidence shows, even if they disagree about the interpretation of that evidence, or the policies that need to be adopted.

... you say that 'Social Trends show that the income of [the poorest 20 per cent of the population] increased by 3 per cent before housing costs.' However, the table from which this figure was selected has other figures which demonstrate the opposite. The table shows that the income of this group, when calculated after housing costs, decreased by 3 per cent. Moreover, you do not refer to the figures in the same table about the rich ...'

(24 May 1994)

Your words

In your answer to **Find out question 2**, include your own summary of the trends shown in tables 6C and 6D (drawing on your answers to the **In detail** questions, and the pie charts you sketched) and comment on the interpretations of the two politicians.

6.3 Find out question 3: Who are the poorest 20%?

FIGURES, FACTS

Chart 6E Economic status: by quintile grouping[1] 1990-1991

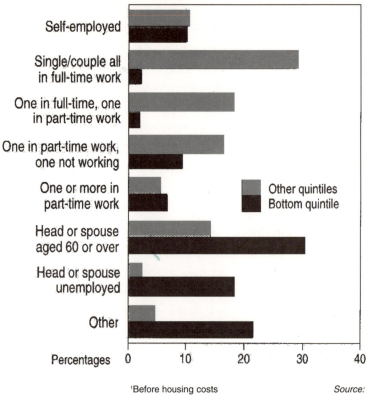

[1] Before housing costs

Source: Department of Social Security

From *Social Trends,* 24 (1994), p. 15.

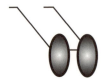

In detail

Note the essential information about the chart: title (note and ponder the footnote), units, location, time period, source.

1 Which economic groups are a) over- b) under-represented in the bottom quintile in relation to other quintile groups? Is this what you would expect?

2 Ask a question that goes beyond the data.

FIGURES, FACTS

Chart 6F Sources of income: by quintile grouping[1], 1990-1991

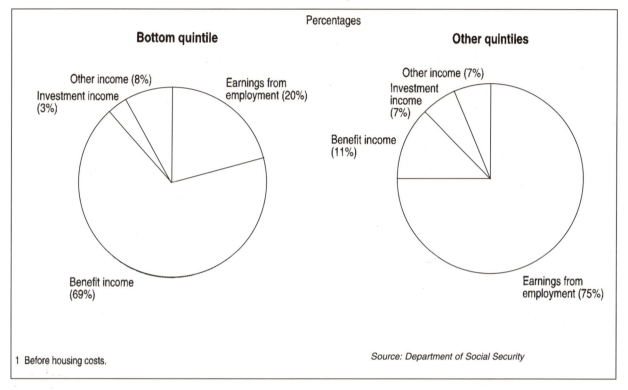

From *Social Trends*, 24 (1994), p. 18.

In detail

Note the five essential points about this chart: title, units, location, time period, source.

1 This chart conveys a clear, simple message. What is it?

2 Are there any other noteworthy details?

3 Ask a question that goes beyond the data.

Figures, facts and interpretation

FIGURES, FACTS

Table 6G — Claimants by benefit entitlement

Thousands

United Kingdom	1978	1983	1988	1989	1990	1991	1992
Men	**879**	**2030**	**1344**	**1062**	**1174**	**1773**	**2073**
UB in payment	347	593	316	191	246	462	478
UB only	268	401	219	123	191	354	370
UB and IS[1]	79	192	97	68	55	108	108
IS only in payment	389	1219	823	717	765	1108	1343
Neither UB nor IS in payment	143	218	205	154	163	202	252
Women	**331**	**855**	**559**	**391**	**384**	**540**	**614**
UB in payment	146	312	184	98	97	164	177
UB only	135	283	166	87	92	153	164
UB and IS	11	29	18	11	5	11	13
IS only in payment	127	384	243	202	204	277	321
Neither UB nor IS in payment	58	158	133	91	83	98	116

1. Income Support replaced Supplementary Benefit from April 1988

Adapted from *Social Security Statistics* (1993).

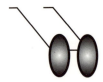

In detail

1. What pattern can you see in the total numbers of a) men b) women claiming benefit?

2. How are these totals made up? Look at the trends in the 'UB in payment' figures, and the 'IS only in payment' figures.

3. Ask a question that goes beyond the data.

4. Draw a graph to show the trends in numbers of people claiming benefit. Decide what you want to show and why you want to show it. You may want to show the total number of claimants; totals of men and women; a breakdown of types of benefit – decide on your message and illustrate it. Make sure your chart is correctly labelled with the five essential information points.

and INTERPRETATION

Chart 6H Male joblessness

Percentage of men, 16–64, non-employed

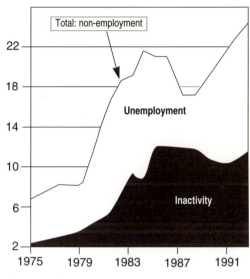

Source: Labour Force Survey

Some words

Anyone focusing on the unemployment figures alone has to agree that the turn-around in the labour market from last January came sooner, and has happened faster, than previous experience would have suggested. But a closer look at the data shows that something curious is going on. Worryingly, it seems that the estimates under-record the unemployment total in terms of the number of people who want to work but do not have a job, and over-record the fall of the last 15 months.

To be sure, claimant unemployment is now 310,000 less than at its December 1992 peak.

But where have the claimants gone? The obvious answer is that they have all found jobs. But statistics show that the number of people in employment – including the self-employed and those on government training schemes – has actually fallen by 58,000 since the end of 1992.

So we have to locate 368,000 people who are no longer employed and no longer draw benefits. They are among the 'economically inactive' – defined by government statisticians as those who are not looking for, or are not available for, work.

(James Nicholson, 'Dole queue masks inactivity', The Guardian, 20 June 1994)

Dear Jean

... The figures you refer to were particularly affected by an increase in the number of self-employed people who report nil or negative incomes ... This finding cannot be interpreted as a fall in living standards, because three quarters of this group spend more than the national average. Moreover, there are marked differences in this group between the reporting of income to the survey and to the Inland Revenue.

(11 April 1994)

Dear Prime Minister

Your point about the self-employed takes little account of changes in the labour market and the grim problems of those endeavouring to set up their own businesses because of losing work as employees. Small wonder that some are using up savings and redundancy money and do not have, or have small future prospect of making, 'profits' to show for their efforts. It is not therefore surprising that the measured incomes of some self-employed after meeting taxes and expenses are very small ...

(24 May 1994)

Your words

In your answer to **Find out question 3**, draw on all the material in this section. You may like to supplement it with, for example, details of the breakdown of spending on or claims for the different types of benefit. *Social Trends* has accessible information on this, and *Social Security Statistics* (from which Table 6G above is derived) is also an informative and well presented publication.

6.4 Find out question 4:
Are some types of family more likely to be poor?

FIGURES, FACTS

Chart 6J Family type: by quintile grouping[1], 1990–1991

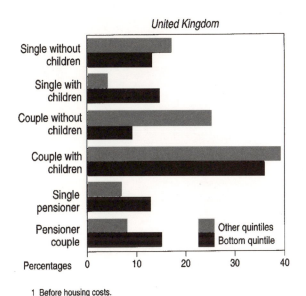

1 Before housing costs.

Source: Department of Social Security

From *Social Trends*, 24 (1994), p. 16.

In detail

Note the five essential points in the chart.

1. Which types of family are a) more b) less c) equally represented in the poorest 20% as compared with the rest of the population?

2. What are the approximate figures for the percentage of lone parents in a) the higher quintile groupings b) the poorest 20%?

3. Ask a question that goes beyond the data.

Chart 6K Families headed by lone mothers and lone fathers as a percentage[1] of all families with dependent children

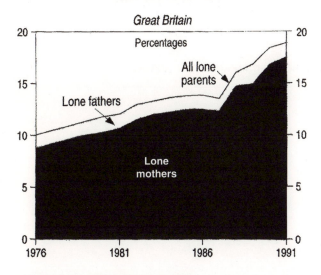

1 3-year moving average used (apart from 1991).

Source: Office of Population Censuses and Surveys

From *Social Trends*, 24 (1994), p. 36.

Some words

Note the five essential points about the chart. Ask yourself some **In detail** questions to focus your understanding of the trends shown.

Below is the commentary from *Social Trends* on the chart. You will note that it makes use of information from the table from which this chart was drawn to supplement the graph.

There were about 1.3 million one-parent families in Great Britain in 1991, containing approximately 2.2 million dependent children. Between 1971 and 1991, one-parent families with dependent children as a proportion of all families with dependent children more than doubled. The rate of increase has quickened in pace recently, mainly due to the increase in lone mothers. In the four years up to 1991 the number of single lone parents grew, increasing by 24 per cent, while the number of dependent children in one-parent families increased by half a million, from 1.7 million in 1987. In 1991 just over 17 per cent of families with dependent children were headed by a lone mother compared with just over 1 per cent headed by a lone father. The figures reflect the rise in both divorce and births outside marriage.

There were nearly 1.2 million lone mothers in Great Britain in 1991, out of a total of nearly 7.2 million mothers.

Figures, facts and interpretation

FIGURES, FACTS

Graph 6L   Families Receiving One-Parent Benefit

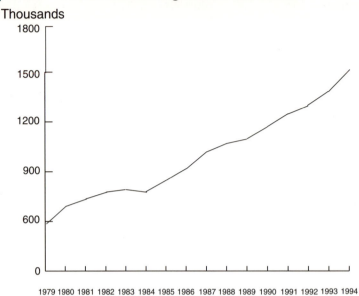

— Total number of children in those families receiving the allowance
  Number of families receiving the allowance

From *Social Security Statistics*, (1991, 1992, 1993, 1994, 1995), DSS.

Activity

1. Add to the graph another line, showing the number of families receiving the allowance, plotted on the following figures. Add your line to the key.

   Number of families receiving One-Parent Benefit in the UK:

1979	1980	1981	1982	1983	1984	1985	1986	1987	1988	1989	1990	1991	1992	1993	1994
381	438	469	508	537	517	576	607	681	708	722	773	818	855	898	941

2. Give the completed chart an appropriate title, and check that the remaining items of essential information are included.

3. Ask yourself three **In detail** questions and record your answers.

56   *Developing Writing – Using Data*

and INTERPRETATION

Dear Jean

... There are now more lone parents than in 1979. Lone parents are overwhelmingly likely to depend on income support, and so are strongly represented in the bottom decile of incomes. The real value of benefit to lone parents has, in fact, increased since 1979. But although lone parents themselves have become better off, their increased representation in the bottom decile reduces the median income of the decile.

(11 April 1994)

Dear Prime Minister

... You go on to suggest two things about lone parent families. You say first that they are better off. But that is to take lone parents at all levels of income, without reference to those in the poorest groups. These are the groups that deserve most attention.

... Second, you refer to the 'increased representation' of lone parents in the bottom decile group. Your advisers seem unaware of DSS figures, which show an increase in this group between 1979 and 1990/91 from 9 to only 10 per cent. This change is so small that it scarcely bears the exaggerated interpretation placed on the matter in your letter ...

(24 May 1994)

Your words

In your answer to **Find out question 4**, draw together your observations about lone parents from the information in this section, and, in your commentary, link it with the extracts from the politicians' correspondence.

Review and report

This brings us to the end of this workshop. I hope you enjoyed it, and learnt something (as I did) about the shape of our society and the perceptions of our politicians. You are now in a position to write a short report in response to the inquiry question. Decide on your who? and why? questions: who might have commissioned it, who will read it, what outcome you would like to see from it? Your question is

Who are the 'weak and vulnerable' in our society? To what extent has the government been successful in protecting these groups over the last 15 years?

Good luck!

6.5 Feedback on activities in Chapter 6

6.1: In detail   Table 6A

1. *Government expenditure, expressed in £billions, has almost doubled between 1981 and 1991. For what this means in 'real terms' and purchasing power, you need to look to your definitions – elsewhere!*

2. *The top six functions listed account for £183.5 billion, about 80%, of the £227.5 billion total spent.*

3. *The increases on these areas were (in descending order): social security, health, education, defence, public order, housing. The biggest proportionate increase was in spending on public order – four times as much in 1991.*

4. *The footnote points you to the government's privatization of the energy industry – evidently it generated a surplus.*

6.1: In detail   Table 6B

1. *The increase over the ten years is £111 billion. It increased by another £25 billion in 1992, a larger increase than in previous years.*

2. *These six major functions accounted for almost 80% (77.7%) of government expenditure in 1991. About £9.8 billion was spent on housing and £29 billion on education. The figures more or less tally with those given in* Social Trends 1993.

3. *No, they do not. Social security, health, public order and education show increases in the size of the slice of government cake allocated to them – albeit a small one (0.5%) in education. Social security shows the largest increase, and public order the largest proportionate increase. Defence and housing show a decline.*

6.2: In detail   Table 6C

1. *Since 1979 the income of the poorest 20% has increased by 3% and the richest 20% by 146%.*

2. *By this measurement, the income of the poorest 20% has declined by 3% and the richest 20% has increased by 155% over the time period.*

3. *The poorest 20% is the only group to have a worse position in 1991 than in 1979. The next bottom quintile has held the same position, while the top three quintiles have improved their position, the top 20% markedly. It seems that the rich were getting richer over the period, and the poor poorer.*

6.3: In detail   Chart 6E

1. *The unemployed, pensioners and 'other' are substantially more heavily represented in the poorest 20%. The proportion of self-employed people in the lowest income band is about the same as in the rest of the population – perhaps surprising. There are more households with at least one member in part-time work than in the rest of the population, but few in full-time work, as would be expected.*

2   *Some questions: in giving a snapshot of one year, a chart like this gives much less information than a table. I'd like to know about the composition of the poorest 20% relative to the sizes of these groups, as compared with previous years. And who is the large group of 'others'? The homeless? The unregistered? The young?*

6.3: In detail   Chart 6F

1   *Roughly speaking, the proportions of income the rest of the population receives from benefits and employment are reversed for the poorest 20%. Income from benefits makes up 69% of the income of the poorest 20%.*

2   *The remaining categories of income, investment and 'other' are not so very different for the poorest 20% of the population. Investment income is likely to be concentrated among the elderly.*

3   *Some questions: which types of benefit to which types of household/family make up the benefit total? Which are growing?*

6.3: In detail   Table 6G

1   *Male claimants for benefit peaked in 1983, before declining towards the end of the eighties. Since then numbers have risen, to reach a new high level in 1992. For women the pattern is similar, but the number of women claimants in 1992 did not reach the peak of 1983.*

2   *In brief, the increase in the total number of claimants lies in the numbers claiming Income Support (IS), not Unemployment Benefit (UB). You might like to speculate on why this should be.*

3   *Some questions: how good a guide to levels of unemployment is the claimant count? Does it, for example, include the groups in the 'other' category of Chart 6F? What caused the marked drop in claimants from 1988 to 1990? Improved employment opportunities? Stringent eligibility tests?*

6.4: In detail   Chart 6J

1   *Pensioners, both couples and single pensioners, and one-parent families are more heavily represented in the bottom 20%. Two-parent families with children have a similar distribution in the bottom 20% as in other quintiles. Single people and couples without children are more likely to be in the higher quintiles.*

2   *Lone parents make up about 15% of the bottom 20% but only 4% of the rest of the population – a marked difference.*

3   *As before, the chart shows a snapshot of the present, not a trend over time, and it would be interesting to see which groups are most likely to live in poverty over a period of time. Has there always been such a concentration of lone parents in the poorest 20%?*

Figures, facts and interpretation

Further reading

Chapman, M. and Mahon, B. (1986). *Plain Figures*. London: HMSO.

Huff, D. (1973). *How to Lie with Statistics*. Harmondsworth: Penguin.

Williams, K. (1989). 'Fact and interpretation', *Study Skills*. London: Macmillan.